Little Books of Guidance

Finding answers to life's big questions!

Also in the series:

What Do We Mean by 'God'? by Keith Ward

How Do I Pray? by John Pritchard

Why Suffering? by Ian S. Markham

What Does It Mean to Be Holy Whole? by Timothy F.
    Sedgwick

What Is Christianity? by Rowan Williams

Who Was Jesus? by James D. G. Dunn

Why Go to Church? by C. K. Robertson

How Can Anyone Read the Bible? by L. William
    Countryman

What Happens When We Die? by Thomas G. Long

What About Sex? by Tobias Stanislas Haller, BSG

HOW TO BE A DISCIPLE AND DIGITAL

A Little Book of Guidance

KAREKIN M. YARIAN

Church Publishing
NEW YORK

Unless otherwise noted, the Scripture quotations contained herein are from the New Revised Standard Version Bible, copyright © 1989 by the Division of Christian Education of the National Council of Churches of Christ in the U.S.A. Used by permission. All rights reserved.

Church Publishing
19 East 34th Street
New York, NY 10016
www.churchpublishing.org

Cover design by Jennifer Kopec, 2Pug Design
Typeset by Progressive Publishing Services

Library of Congress Cataloging-in-Publication Data

A record of this book is available from the Library of Congress.

ISBN-13: 978-1-64065-017-6 (pbk.)
ISBN-13: 978-1-64065-018-3 (ebook)

Printed in the United States of America

Contents

About the Author

Br. Karekin Madteos Yarian is an author and social activist from San Francisco, and is a member of the Episcopal religious community known as the Brotherhood of Saint Gregory since 1994. Karekin is also the Brother Protector of the Companions of Dorothy the Worker, an ecumenical religious community dedicated to ministry in the queer community in San Francisco.

Karekin is the subject of the award-winning documentary "Changing Habits" by Sara Needham, and has appeared in the nationally released via media series produced by Every Voice Network, an advocacy organization in the Episcopal Church for progressive causes.

Karekin's work in San Francisco includes spiritual advocacy for members of the transgender and broader queer community and political activism for the disenfranchised. Karekin is a Spiritual Director, and works in a variety of ministries in support of the Gospel mandate to care for the "least of these." Online Karekin is known as PunkMonk, San Francisco.

Introduction

Social media has become a largely inescapable virtual world in which all manner of human social groups are being formed. The ease with which we can stay informed about our families and friends has made social media an indispensable tool. In addition, the ability to connect across the globe with others who share our interests, our faith, and our love of all things kitten-ish has created networks of social relationship unimaginable before the advent of platforms such as Twitter and Facebook.

Among these, there have been wonderful virtual communities created and centered on prayer, faith, and spirituality. It doesn't take a long search before we find social media presences for our Episcopal Church, its dioceses, parishes, and groups, and pages for nearly every ministry in which the Church engages. Hashtags on Twitter make it easy to stay informed and meet others in active ministry.

There are many benefits to using social media as a tool for community building, including the global nature of the platform, the possibility of real-time interaction and conversation, and the discovery of multicultural points of view and shared values. But within the social media space, issues of attentiveness versus distraction, self-assertion, consumption, and anonymity have provided challenges in setting boundaries and maintaining healthy community. How does our discipleship as Christians speak to these challenges? Can the model of Christian discipleship offer a rudimentary framework for an ethics of social media community to help foster the growth and stability of spiritual communities online? And more importantly, how do our responsibilities as Christians come into play as we navigate the good and the not so good of social media interaction? In short . . . how can we practice discipleship in a digital world?

1

The Landscape

The World Wide Web has become a tangled skein indeed. No longer is it just a matter of e-mail and websites. Many parishes not only have to contend with keeping a web page up to date or managing an e-mail list for newsletter distribution—now they must also manage a social media presence and try to keep it informative, engaging, and current. And for many of us, we now live in a world of notifications and friend requests, Twitter feeds, and Facebook likes. It can seem a lot to manage, and what was once just a means of keeping up with cousins and school friends and enjoying the photos from Maris and Julie's trip to Hawaii has for many morphed into an entertaining, distracting, and occasionally maddening stream of words, videos, news articles, information (some true and some not true), and catchy "memes" that manage to convey the angst of the day.

Facebook today has nearly 1.8 billion users. That is as large as the largest of countries—a nation unto itself. Twitter has about 328 million active users a month . . . as large as the population of the United States. A proliferation of apps, micro-blogging platforms, and social media tools for mobile devices means that we are almost always connected to a steady flow of information and updates from those near and far—those we know well and those we barely know but for a friend request or a follow on Twitter.

With the click of a button, we can upload a photo to Instagram or a video to YouTube or Vimeo; share our thoughts on the news of the day on Twitter; or share a prayer, an inspirational quote, or a righteous rant about the next door neighbor's howling dog. Likewise, with a quick click we can share with our friends something posted by someone else, share our opinion regarding another person's dinner choices or politics, and contribute to the viral explosion of a news story that has been proven false. As I am usually prone to say when a celebrity death is incorrectly announced sometimes long after their actual death, "I hear it's often easier the second time around." Even worse is when they haven't died at all—we get caught up in another celebrity hoax only to be told an hour later that Boris Karloff is in fact alive and well and just vacationing in Palm Springs.

For all of this, the complicated landscape of social media is as true a means of fostering community as any other. And for those of us that experience social media as another "location" in which to live our lives in Christian discipleship, there are some unique benefits. There are also some unique problems. And it is to both of these that we now turn.

On January 12, 2010, an earthquake with a magnitude of 7.3 struck the island nation of Haiti. It killed nearly a quarter of a million people. Episcopal Relief and Development was one of the first NGOs to begin raising money and relief for the devastated nation. The outpouring of prayer and the fundraising efforts quickly began to proliferate within Episcopal circles on social media. The response was like lightning, and the Christian witness to care for our neighbors was startling. The American Red Cross raised nearly half a billion dollars online, and the total amount raised through fundraising and donations globally reached

$13.5 billion for the aid of the Haitian people. Episcopal Relief and Development raised several millions of dollars. It was a staggering response. There are countless other instances in recent years where social media has been used as a platform to coordinate our response as people of faith in the context of the Episcopal Church.

As events unfold across the world—whether terrorist attacks overseas or in our own backyard, protest movements, close elections in contested races, or the latest gaffe by a celebrity—social networks seem to be one of the first places we check to see what folks are saying or to share our own thoughts. We can instantly express solidarity with people across the globe, share in the sorrows of friends and neighbors, and increasingly (on platforms like Facebook) donate money to help someone with medical expenses or support political and social causes dear to our hearts.

In today's digital landscape, we can engage in real-time conversations with someone literally on the other side of the world. In my years on social media, I have made "friends" with individuals across Europe, South America, the Middle East, and Africa. Whether during the mass rallies against the former President of Brazil, the aftermath of terrorist attacks in Istanbul or Manchester, or attacks against Christians in Pakistan, I have followed the wisdom and work of clergy, aid workers, and activists in *real time* as they minister and work among the suffering, the wounded, and the fearful. I can lend my encouragement, my network, and my own social media presence to aid in disseminating information, raising money, and expressing solidarity. The massive web of interconnections made possible in social media means that its power often rivals or bests traditional news media. The global nature of social media platforms flies in the face of populists and demagogues who would divide us from one another. We become acutely aware of the power of this capacity for exchange only when we learn that some social media platforms have been banned and walled off from certain repressive nations for whom this kind of access to free ideas poses a real threat. The manipulation of news media on social platforms has proven a powerful tool for repressive governments to sway public opinion in very localized ways. Hack-tivists, dissidents, extremists, and resistance workers have used social networks for both good and ill because of the ease of transmitting information quickly and directly.

If Facebook or Twitter were a nation, it would be one of the most diverse, globally oriented, and probably neurotic nations on earth. Yet in the midst of this great swirl of information and connection, we bring our Christian selves. Much like in the nondigital world, we can be as private or as public about our faith as we dare. Aside from bringing our day-to-day lives and experiences, our sense of humor, and our opinions, we can and often do bring our prayer requests and testimonies. Many of us find, read, and share sermons from our preaching friends, and we type (or not) a thousand "amens" in agreement with memes that proclaim God's goodness. We, in fact, evangelize. We accumulate followers and friends, and we send friend requests to those whose faith we admire—who share our values and interests in matters of following Jesus as authentically we can.

Yet, we can just as easily unfollow and unfriend those with whom we find ourselves in disagreement, especially in these partisan and polarizing times. After the agonizing animosity of the 2016 electoral season, there are likely many more of us than we would like to admit who have conflated social media connections with actual relationships and too easily discarded the former to the detriment of the latter. Some of the damage is still being repaired. And some of that damage is likely lasting.

But, like it or not, social media networks are here to stay, and the capacity for sharing in good works and the Good News is profoundly magnified by an increasing global network that allows for the quick and easy exchange of ideas and inspiration. So how do we, as Christian people, engage with others on social media in a way that honors both our faith and witness to the teachings of Christ and the promises made in baptism—especially when the ease of social media interactions brings with it a number of pitfalls that can quickly challenge us to live up to our best intentions as people of faith?

2

The Challenges—and the Opportunities

Reason #1 to be an Episcopalian . . . no matter what you believe there's bound to be at least one Episcopalian who agrees with you.

Robin Williams

Aside from all of the benefits of social media, there are a number of profound issues associated with the nature and quality of our interactions in a digital space that can leave us profoundly unsettled. We've all experienced them, and they can be maddening. Facebook, Twitter, and other platforms for social connection are technologies that we love and we hate—and that we sometimes love to hate and hate to love. Who among us hasn't contemplated taking time away or quitting altogether, only to return some time later because we miss the interaction, the ease with which we stay in touch with friends and family, and the sometimes marvelous capacity for distraction and connection? Some of the difficulties in the social media landscape are obvious, but I want to explore them a bit deeper than just listing the frustrations that we've all experienced.

The first issue is a question about the nature of relationships. What distinguishes a purely social network–oriented relationship from a real-world one? When the word "friend" is used less as an indicator of friendship than as a game-ification strategy by a social media platform to foster connections that are used to make money for a company, it muddies the waters for the individual about just what constitutes "friendship," and gives an impression of authentic relationship by hiding the transactional profit motive that underlies the exchange between two or more people using the platform. I want to explore this idea of game-ification a bit because many social media platforms have adopted this model to grow their businesses and attract users. What this literally means is that social media networks are constructed to work like a game that rewards players for accumulating "friends" and "followers" and "likes." Like a competitive sport or a board game, "likes" and "shares" occupy the same mental space as "points"—and the resulting feeling of reward for gathering them act on the brain in much the same way winning a competition does. They provide us with stimuli that mimic the ways that reward and punishment affect the pleasure centers of our brain.

The result of this game strategy produces something new. We end up with a wide variety of "friends" on social media who we don't actually know in real life. The sum of what we know about them is controlled by profiles, privacy settings, and an affirming collection of clicks, likes, and comments. Whether there is the possibility of developing real friendships with many of the "friends" or "followers" we have collected is unknown because there is no basis for actual relationship beyond that which is enabled (or inhibited) by the social media network that connects us. How many times have we seen a post by a friend or colleague who has publicly stated their intention to "unfriend" a great number of people in order to make their social network more manageable?

"If you're reading this, then congratulations! You made the cut." There's that game strategy again. "Whew . . . I'm glad I wasn't unfriended!" The hit to my serotonin levels feels so good. But the mere fact is that words like "unfriending" have become a part of our modern lexicon, giving rise to the question, What is the nature of social media friendship? Are these people or are they just points?

What of those people with whom we are both real-life friends and also social media "friends?" Where are the boundaries between those two ways of being in relationship with one another? It may seem like an easy question, but it can be quite complex in the digital space we inhabit. Why does it hurt when someone we don't know "unfriends" us? And when someone we know in real life "unfriends" us on social media, why do we suddenly feel as though our relationship with them outside of social media is somehow irreparably harmed? There is no clearer picture of the hurts and bruises made possible by this cavalier treatment of "friendship" that defies the truths of friendship that we already know. There is something quite disturbing and also quite amusing when we speak of "unfriending" our family . . . as though it were that simple to discard relationships based on the perspectives we glean only from social media. We have been tricked into thinking that the product truly represents the person. This speaks volumes about our radically changed perspective created by our participation in this new digital landscape. If the world is not the Kingdom we await, then how much less so is the digital world of social media and its algorithms that let us see each other only in the way that serves a business' profit margin? And who are we in this new world, as Christians and as individuals committed to demonstrating the love of God . . . especially in an arena that sometimes sorely tests our patience?

Social media networks encourage us to speak out and assert ourselves and our opinions. It gives us a platform for saying what we think or feel and for sharing the minutia of our days, our visceral reactions to events of note, and our faith, should we choose. Social media gives us license to share ourselves thoughtfully or impulsively, emotionally, or in ways that can seem detached. It leaves us at the mercy of interpretation by those who don't know us well enough to understand what we're thinking or what informs our thinking. It's difficult to be clear and articulate on complex issues in 140 characters or less. And yet, there are many of us who have convinced ourselves that such is possible. But this is caricature, not character.

The game-ification of reaction and response on social media convinces us that our opinions matter. Or that they should matter to both those who know us and to those who do not. And that others' opinions should, likewise, matter to us. When response is based on reaction rather than thought, conversation, and relationship, then the possibility of misrepresentation of who we are is vastly increased. And so is the prospect of argument and dissatisfaction.

I say this often, and sometimes it makes people upset. Other times it makes people curious, and every once in a while, someone will say "OH! Of course!" But the truth of the matter is that our opinions matter to really very few people. Especially in the social media landscape. Why should a relative stranger on social media care if I disagree with something they've posted? They may love that I enjoy cooking or that we share a fondness for a particular YouTube singer, but when someone posts their opinion on an issue of the day, why should they care that I disagree? Especially if they haven't asked for my opinion?

This is important. Not every expression of an opinion on social media is an invitation for my disagreement— or even for my agreement for that matter. And it isn't just because they may not care. It may be that the decision to express my feelings on social media was just that—a desire to express. Not an attempt at conversation, not an invitation to debate. In fact, it may be nothing more than an opportunity to vent my frustration, to express my surprise, or just because I was bored and had nothing better to do than say what I felt about something I just read.

The opportunity for millions upon millions of people to express themselves and their thoughts via social media is a delightful innovation. It gives us an opportunity to understand the breadth of human feeling and even different interpretations of an event that are culturally based and sometimes religiously informed. The dark side of this is that when we become convinced that our opinions matter too much, we take uninvited opportunities to express disagreement where our input wasn't asked for.

Don't be tempted to say "if you post publicly, then I have every right to express my thoughts." That's simply not true. Nor is it our responsibility to begin with the assumption that our social media friends haven't rationally and reasonably come to their opinions and therefore need our correction when they haven't even asked for it.

For example, most people don't really understand the nature of privacy on a platform like Facebook, such as what is shared publicly versus what is shared with "friends" versus "close friends" or even how to share a post that is only seen by a few people that we have selected—these ways of managing privacy are barely understood, not widely used well to manage who sees what we've posted, and change frequently. So also is the distinction between one's "wall" and one's "news feed." If someone posts on my wall, then I see that as equivalent to someone coming into my living room for a chat. The newsfeed, on the other hand, is the equivalent of the public square or town hall. And often it is indiscriminate—except to the Facebook algorithm—in what is shown there. This is largely because we haven't gone to the effort to categorize the numerous connections we have, and the algorithms involved don't follow any logic that we understand, presenting us with whatever the platform thinks will be most likely to engender a reaction.

Facebook pages and groups are another way of managing community interaction. Pages and groups are a marvelous way to creating conversation around topics of specific interest, engaging with public figures we know and like, and organizing around issues that are important to us. Pages and groups, thankfully, have moderators or administrators that set guidelines for community interaction. Sadly, they're not always enforced, or they can sometimes be selectively enforced. As an example, I have long managed a social media page on Facebook for religious brothers and sisters in a variety of communities and traditions. It is intended to share our thoughts, prayers, reflections, and the challenges of living the religious life with one another in a supportive environment. It is not intended for the sharing of news articles, memes, pictures, videos, or other such posts without some information about why it is relevant to the poster and why it might be interesting to those in the group.

Here is what our guidelines say:

Our group is intended to be a place of conversation, not merely the consumption of information. As such, there are a few expectations about what is appropriate in this space. Our moderators are very good at helping the conversation to remain respectful and open.

Please practice charity, kindness, and forbearance.

Please refrain from politics, debate, and disparagement.

Please do not cross post links from other groups or websites unless you are willing to share what about that information is meaningful to you and why you think it may interest others in the group. The [group], unlike other Facebook groups, is not a clearinghouse for information that can be readily found elsewhere. It is instead an ongoing conversation about our experiences or reflections on living the religious life.

When new folks join, please make every effort to welcome them.

Should you choose to depart, please say farewell so that we can thank you for your time with us.

While you are here, share freely of your own experiences with others so that we may all grow in faith and witness. Hold one another in prayer. And share with one another in the peace of Christ.

Your Moderators

Are these perfect guidelines? Not by any stretch. But they have surely gone a long way to ensure that what people share in the group are not opportunities for disagreement, disparagement, or hostility. Yes . . . even religious folks can be that way. Also, commonly used in the group is a strategy for inviting conversation such as "I welcome your thoughts on this" or "Tell me about your experiences with this." This is a clear way of letting people know that we are looking for conversation, even respectful disagreement, or the sharing of experiences that have led others to different conclusions than our own.

Another challenge altogether too common on social media platforms is that we have a tendency—especially in polarizing times or around controversial issues—to reinforce our own biases by self-selection. Nowhere was this more clear than the frenzy of "unfriending" and "unfollowing" that happened during the 2016 campaign and election season. The vast reshaping of networks of friends, family members, and colleagues will require a lengthy period of recovery. It is not only the damage to relationships that proves troubling: It is also the creation of virtual "gated communities" where the only ones left in our social networks are those whose opinions and ideas closely align with our own—or at the very least don't challenge them.

Perhaps it is a good thing that we don't see social media platforms as the only location where we may have conversations that are difficult. Maybe we are inclined to meet face to face with folks with whom we disagree so that we may learn to honor one another in spite of those disagreements. However, I suspect that this greatly diminishes our opportunities to understand issues more globally and experience the views of others with whom our social media connection may be the only chance to meet or hear a viewpoint that differs from our own. This vacuum left behind by virtual compartmentalizing creates a lost opportunity to learn how to be in conversation and relationship with others. And it makes it increasingly likely that we will respond less charitably the next time we come across a viewpoint that challenges our own.

How do we foster relationships with one another on a social media platform when we have to express ourselves in 140 characters or less? How do we learn to listen to one another when the easiest way to respond to someone is by clicking a "reaction" button that eliminates the need to say anything at all? Are we really expressing our own selves when a simple "re-tweet" of someone else's words not only implies our agreement, but further amplifies a single thought without almost no effort on our part?

This is not to imply that social media connections using the model of "shares," re-tweets," "likes," and "favorites" aren't fun and useful in their own regard. I do suspect that they give the *impression* that we're being relational, that we're engaging with one another and conversing, when in fact we're really not. At its best, this model provides us with quick ways to disseminate information, say what we think, and appear to share in the joys, trials, and interests of a good many people we may or may not have met. At its worst, however, it can be nothing more than an endless assertion of ourselves punctuated by a limited palette of reactions and the ability to amplify to untold degrees things that merely reinforce our own biases. And I'm not entirely sure that for followers of Jesus this constitutes what it means to truly be in relationship with others.

What does it mean to find avenues for relationship *beyond the platform*? I have found countless opportunities to grab coffee with folks I have only met on social media, to visit them when I'm in their cities, to pop into their churches when I am on vacation, or to invite them to events of import in my own world. I have known social media acquaintances who have held potluck events with folks they have met through pages and groups, and I have met folks who have started new companies with ideas and people they have encountered on a social media network. I even recently attended an art exhibit based on an Instagram tag that a group of local artists coordinated.

The capacity to form amazing alliances and creative endeavors is enormous on social media. Far from merely an opportunity to connect with old friends and acquaintances, it represents a powerful platform for forging new ones. As Christian people, the ability to share and proclaim the Gospel and to foster new means of community is amazing. As a religious under vows, I have first-hand experience in creating and sustaining bonds of affection among a variety of folks in religious life—in communities around the globe—all bound by a common desire to love and serve God and one another.

3

The Dark Side

There is a dark underbelly to the internet—all of it—and social media networks are no exception. In fact, they are sometimes a whirlpool of opportunities for us to engage in bad behavior. Even the bad behavior we decry on other parts of the internet. We all know what "trolls" are—those denizens of the net that hold forth as their solemn duty the creation of hostility, argument, and character assassination. Trolls see no benefit in attacking issues. They attack people. Sadly, trolling has now become an activity that any of us are capable of engaging in whether we know we're doing it or not. And many of us have done so without even realizing it.

The following are some of the behaviors we see online and that many of us have even picked up in social media interactions that fall into the category of trolling:

- Insults and accusations
- Persistent debates
- Criticizing grammar (or spelling)
- Insisting on being constantly offended
- Being a know-it-all
- Profanity and yelling
- Exaggeration
- Speaking off topic
- Spamming

Other behaviors that don't necessarily fall into the category of trolling but that greatly diminish the quality of our possible social interactions and the responsible public square that we hope to create include:

- Sharing fake news
- Ghosting (disappearing from an interaction or conversation without explanation)
- Chain letter posts
- Oversharing (posting inappropriate personal details not suitable for public arenas)
- Vague-booking (posting something vague that begs for reaction)

- Inappropriate tagging
- Unattributed or permission-less sharing

Trolling and other inappropriate behaviors diminish the overall quality of dialogue. They are often the behaviors that make us lament social media and consider checking out. Some of these behaviors are entirely offensive and disrespectful, and most of them rely on the fact that—unlike in face-to-face interactions—there is no ability to gauge how our words and actions will affect those on the receiving end. This virtual "wall" shields us from many of the consequences we might reasonably expect in real-life encounters. So behaviors that might be mitigated otherwise are given license to take root in ways that we ourselves may not even be aware of. It ends up, sometimes, being a race to the bottom of what would be acceptable in real social encounters and authentic relationships.

We may see ourselves as being responsible for pointing out flaws in an argument or asserting our disagreement or our own offended-ness. We may inadvertently (or, God forbid, even deliberately) make insinuations or accusations about someone's level of education or privilege or make assumptions about a person's experiences and abilities that are not our business to make. This is facilitated by the echo chamber of our own self-assertion that is fostered by "unreal" nature of social media and the virtual wall between our computer screens that remove most of the consequences that we would normally face for making such assumptions to a person's face. When confronted with someone's anger on social media, it is impossible for us to see whether what we have said or done has caused them either hurt or fear that led to their anger. All we experience is the monolith of their upset and a poor venue in which to assure or assuage the person whose feelings we have hurt.

So what are we as Christian disciples to do when it comes to social media's potential for living out our gospel mandate to love one another? How do we show the best of ourselves and our faith tradition in the morass that is social media? What behavior is appropriate for us who wish to demonstrate our faith and our lives as followers of Jesus?

4

A Beginning Framework for Digital Discipleship

One of the first ways we can address the joys and pitfalls of social media communication and digital discipleship requires a shift in the way we view these interactions. We must move away from the idea that our social media presence is about the consumption of information and instead look at it as a conversation. We need to begin humanizing these interactions. All of the information presented to us on newsfeeds and Twitter streams is not created equal. Nor are the motives underlying what is highlighted for our attention, and the responsibilities we have in responding to the real human beings that present themselves, their lives and concerns, to us in expectation of authentic engagement.

News articles, advertisements, and viral posts need to be teased apart from, and handled differently than, the check-ins, posts, and thoughts of our social media friends who share them. The latter require (or at least deserve) the opportunity to be treated differently—more humanely—than sources that are seeking to only drive the profits of news agencies and information clearinghouses and corporations looking to sell us something. The commodification of our posts by platforms such as Twitter and Facebook sometimes makes it difficult to remember that those we choose to call our friends in the social media space are qualitatively different from companies that use our information to drive profits. But our Christian responsibility is to distinguish between them and to remember the honor and dignity of their personhood as we interact with them.

The issue of personhood is of great importance here, so I'd like to explore that a little more. At the beginning of this book, we spoke a bit about not every social media post being intended to invite our critique or even our commentary. Sometimes people just want to share things about their day or their thoughts and maybe even enjoin the prayers of their social media friends.

Recalling the baptismal promise to respect the dignity of every human person, we must begin with the exercise of remembering the *personhood* on the other end of the words, posts, and shares that come across our newsfeed. This obliges us to remember the complexity of human beings, not reducing them as individuals to having the same worth as other sources of information that flow across our newsfeeds. This means appreciating contradictions, differences, and subtleties that are impossible to convey in a short amount of space. It means remembering that people are often more nuanced in their thoughts than what they have written. And it means remembering that all of these caveats apply to our own selves. So, the capacity for self-reflection is important. How many times have any of us dashed off a quick post only to have its meaning or intent wildly misunderstood by nearly everyone who reads it? How many times have any of us intended a quick bit of sarcasm only to have it taken seriously, offending people unintentionally?

While social media seems to encourage quickly and easily sharing everything from funny memes to news articles, this ease also encourages a lack of critical discernment of our intentions in sharing. No one questions whether a cute cat video is intended to make people smile, but strong and unequivocal statements about public figures and celebrities, highly partisan articles on social issues, and highly charged rants dashed off without thinking or without commentary as to why we are sharing it can result in a whole lot of social media anxiety and drama. The point is not to stop sharing these things, but to consider why we are sharing and what kind of response we are looking for. To be clear.

There are a couple of helpful tools we can use to make our intentions clear and to not invite or create offense. For example, by stating "I invite your own thoughts and opinions on this," we are actually inviting conversation. Conversely, we are free to say "I'm not looking for feedback on this post," and we can say clearly, "I know some folks will disagree with this, and that's fine" to make space and mitigate the impulse for disagreements to take root.

We can pay attention to the list of trolling behaviors above and remember not to participate in them. We can also set boundaries through the use of pinned posts on our timelines or in groups we manage to spell out the expectations for those who wish to post there. Be clear on where your boundaries actually are and enforce them. On my own Facebook author's page or my personal Facebook page, I am clear that my friends can disrespect me (although I would rather they didn't) but can never disrespect others when commenting on a post I've written. I will gladly delete threads hijacked by trolling people, whose dialogue has descended into outrage, or whose participants are no longer listening to each other. As a Christian person, and as a person whose stewardship of my social media space is my own responsibility, I choose to not contribute to that level of dialogue. I will private message troublemakers and politely ask them to stop, and if they persist in behaving badly, I will unfriend them and even block them, though in many years on social media the number of folks I've blocked is barely a handful. In addition, I will offer apologies privately by message or e-mail rather than hash it out in a public thread or feed. Though most of my own posts on Facebook are set as "public," I have my privacy settings set in such a way that not everyone can post on my wall. And no one may tag me in a post or photo without my ability to review it first. When someone posts on my Facebook wall, I can review it and either allow it on my wall or "hide" it. Sometimes I hide it even if I like it because it may be a re-post of something I have already posted or someone has tagged me in a "share" of something I have posted. No one needs to see something I have already posted a dozen more times.

Since we are "curators" or stewards of our own social media presence, we have a responsibility to be mindful of the tone we set, the boundaries we create, and the expectations of interaction between anyone invited to come into our space.

Remembering the virtual wall between our screens, there is a great likelihood that we have a few (or many) social media connections with people we have never met in real life. The only thing they may, in fact, know about us is what our social media feeds reflect—which is utterly lacking in context of what makes us the human beings that we are. There is not much information on our histories, experiences, or the values that shape us that can serve as a lens for people through which they may read what we say on social media. Does that article we share reflect what we value? Does that response to a disagreement demonstrate our better selves? And how do these reflect on our faith?

Getting back to personhood, we have to remember the great diversity of voices and values behind the information that pours across our social media feeds. Because social media platforms are global in scale, we are presented with many opinions and thoughts that differ substantially from our own. As we have also come to learn, the capacity for manipulation of public opinion is very high on social media. We are only just beginning to unpack the ubiquity of "fake news" and the unimaginable new world of "alternative facts." It is therefore essential for those who wish to bring an authentic Christian discipleship to our social media presence to exercise discernment and, above all, patience. This means contributing to dialogues on social media in ways that are mindful and respectful, not to be the purveyors of false information, not to manufacture outrage, and always to give others the benefit of the doubt. It means understanding that not all things on a social media feed are of equal value, and that much has little to no value. Part of responsible social media use is to discern what does have value and to respond accordingly; to understand that this value is largely found in the potential for loving, relational encounters with other human beings of rich variety, complexity, and dignity; and to remember that people are worth more than their opinions on one issue or another and that they, too, have been formed in the image of God and are worthy of all dignity and respect even in the midst of a disagreement.

As a spiritual director for over twenty years, one of the models I bring to my encounters with others is an understanding that there is always a third party in our conversations—God's Holy Spirit, which is present and available in love and commitment. The Spirit is there to teach us; to open each of us up to opportunities for growth and learning; and to guide us into right relationships with God, the world, and others. This means a relationship of presence, self-giving, forgiveness, and openness to transformation. It is this perspective that I try to bring to my social media interactions.

Much as we might be tempted to chuckle at or dismiss the idea of *God as an observer* in our social media culture, it is only because of the diminishment of authentic relationships in that culture that we might find this laughable. As dedicated Christ followers, we shouldn't be so quick to dismiss the idea. Communication of any real and lasting value throughout human history has been mindful of the power and impact of words and images for good or ill. They have the capacity to reveal truths about the speaker and to link us together in common human experience. Words and images can inspire, shock, create, and destroy. And whether we are writers, orators, preachers, poets, or diarists, for most of human history the power of words to do these things has been understood and has enjoined us to use them wisely and purposefully, even *if* our intent is to challenge others. Somehow, with the technological advances of digital communication available to us, we seem to have forgotten the import of words and their power. Social media too often encourages us to use words and images uncritically or thoughtlessly, and communication has become so casual that often we aren't really "communicating" at all as much as proliferating words and images without regard to their objective value.

Christ as the *Word* of God challenges us as disciples to see the truth of that *Word* as the metric against which the truthiness and value of all other words should be measured. God as Observer puts us in mind of this ever-present *Word* that seeks to bring all of us into an authentic relationship characterized by the values taught by Jesus Christ; a relationship of wholeness and reconciliation; one of healing. And so, remembering that the world between our screens, while virtual, still belongs to God is a good way to gauge whether what you are about to say, share, or post is of value, whether it is just a sweet puppy video to brighten someone's day or a rant about whether it is better to use a bulletin versus a prayer book for worship (followed by my favorite tag: </snark>).

The list of words we could use as Christian disciples is practically endless when it comes to what we should aspire to. It is easy to parrot the best of these words over and again without paying too much attention to them when it comes to our choices on social media. Of course, our words should demonstrate love, mercy, and kindness. We should speak to justice, faith, and our ever-present—though sometimes challenged—Christian hope. We should be prone to forgive faults and offenses as we wish to be forgiven. And we should stand on the side of the poor, marginalized, and oppressed; welcome the alien; and comfort the bereaved. We should be truthful. I'd like to challenge us to root our budding ethics of social media in a set of words that may provide us with fresh insight into how we can be better digital disciples.

The rule of the religious community to which I belong enumerates six virtues that I find to be helpful as a framework for social interaction of any kind. I find them a particularly useful starting point as an ethic for social media interactions and as a way to foster exchanges that honor those I encounter. These virtues are *quietness, patience, humility, charity, courage,* and *prayer*. It is these same terms that my beloved brothers and sisters in the Gregorian tradition use to speak about how we serve as witnesses of Our Redeemer's love so that "those persons who may come to know [us] may by [our] example be brought the Good News of the Gospel of Jesus Christ." (The Rule of the Brotherhood of Saint Gregory)

Quietness

Christians are not called to be silent in the face of injustice. This is not our vocation. It is good to take a stand in the face of oppression, marginalization, and the needs of the poor and outcast. Social media is as good a place to take a stand as any community of which we are a part. In fact, it can be argued that social media networks and platforms like Twitter and Facebook give us a unique opportunity to bear witness to our faith's commitment to issues of justice. However, our faith—particularly the spirit of devotion and prayer—also asks us to engage the world with gentleness. It is this spirit of quietness that we are speaking of here.

There have been many times when it has proven to be of great benefit for many to remain in quietness while the world rages around them. Sometimes the capacity for outrage, argument, and dissent on social media provides us with a rich opportunity to listen, but not every post is an invitation for our point of view, and we should not have something to say on every topic or issue.

I have learned a great deal about human experience, the occasionally profound wisdom of groups, and the differences between healthy conversation and unhealthy communication by sitting back and watching a discussion unfold. I have seen people mend divides as often as they create them. I have watched people make insightful observations, share their personal stories, and make space for disagreement in deeply respectful ways. All, thankfully and unsurprisingly, without any input from me! I have learned a great deal from many people on my social media network, many of whom I would never have had the opportunity to know or appreciate without the connections available in the digital world.

Quietness means being willing to step aside from the self-assertion promoted by social media and allow others to engage in conversation. Quietness means not encouraging our ego to assert itself, but to be open to learning from the wisdom and experiences of others. It is, perhaps, even stepping into the world between screens where God's Spirit as Observer also waits in quietness and appreciating the breadth of human commitment and dedication to conversation and the hope of deeper relationships through mutual understanding. The exercise of quietness is a fundamental starting place for a Christian ethic of social media.

Patience

The book of Proverbs reminds us that "hot tempers cause arguments, but patience brings peace" (Prov. 15:18). To exercise patience as a Christian virtue in social media, let's start at the beginning. To post or not to post?

It can be a useful practice to wait before dashing off a post, a comment, or an article when our emotions run high regarding the subject. Social media can be an echo chamber for outrage . . . we've all experienced that. Because digital platforms make it so easy, we often leap into the machinery of outrage and accusation too quickly. Even unintentionally. Patience requires us to step back and ask ourselves about the value of what we are about to share or say and whether it will contribute to or detract from an authentic conversation about the issue at hand. There is no harm in waiting.

Patience as a practice can also help us avoid some of the more egregious faux pas on social media, such as sharing fake news, celebrity death hoaxes, and other verifiably false information as well as click bait-y web links and even viruses. Before indulging the impulse to widely share a bit of news or a web link, take the time to verify its truth. By now everyone ought to know about websites like snopes.com (a debunking website) or the miraculous oracle called Google. It takes a bit of extra time, but if we as Christians act as proper stewards of our own social media contributions, we can go a long way toward cleaning up some of the worst elements of the digital landscape.

Humility

If we are capable of stepping back and acknowledging that we have sometimes have nothing useful to contribute to a conversation, then we begin to approach humility as a virtue for social media. But it is more than that—it is also the recognition of the vast number of things we don't know, can't say with certainty, or are outside our areas of expertise.

As a white person, I do not have a complete understanding of the experiences and internal struggles of people of color, women, and many other oppressed individuals. So a good starting place is to let others speak for themselves. The reality of instantly available information is not the same as knowledge. It is not our place to speak on subjects when other more qualified people can do so, and we should recognize that we often do *not* know enough about a particular topic to publically express an opinion. This is where humility can open our eyes to a vast variety and diversity of points of view. We can learn from others, and humility gives us license to do so. Humility recognizes, in spite of our current cultural climate, that not all opinions are of equal value— even, often, our own.

Humility in the social media landscape allows us to say things like "I'm sorry" or "I don't know" in ways that contribute to more positive dialogue. Humility also demands that we choose when we engage and when we remain silent in regard to current issues, arguments, or conflicts on social media, and it allows us to act as healers and bridge builders rather than dividers and vessels for outrage.

Charity

Charity is one of the most recognizable virtues espoused in scriptures, and it is one of the most helpful when it comes to engaging in healthy communication and relationships with others, most especially with those who are different from us.

Charity is understanding. While it sees things as they are, it refuses to accept that people cannot break free of the systems they inhabit. It exercises generosity of spirit and refuses physical or rhetorical violence even toward the oppressor, which is, of course, what Christ commanded when he said "Resist not evil." (Matt. 5:39) Charity as a strategy for Christian discipleship on social media gives those whom we encounter the freedom to express themselves as they are and as they wish without our correction.

Charity is about building relationships and extending to one another the benefit of the doubt. It is about recognizing when there is no intent to offend and acknowledging the limits of human knowledge and understanding—the complexity of life—without expecting every person to perceive or express nuance.

There is no need, therefore, to leap to admonishing people for failing to clearly communicate or to correct the point of view they have arrived at through their own experiences however much it differs from our own. When I comment on someone else's post, am I being charitable? The virtue of charity is linked closely to self-offering, not the offering of an opinion, an alternative point of view, or our indignation in the place of our loving presence.

Can we as Christian disciples offer ourselves in relationship on social media in a way that is characterized by a self-giving love? Can we be encouragers instead of admonishers? Can we celebrate those with whom we disagree as being entitled to self-expression? Charity insists that differences in opinion don't equal differences in human value and dignity. So in exercising charity as a social media value, we are called to build community, not to tear it down, and to seek to undo the many ways in which we are encouraged to separate ourselves into silos of self-affirming viewpoints and to offer an alternative to the atomization of endless self-assertions. Charity invites others to do likewise.

Courage

Courage as a Christian virtue on social media invites *witness*. Courage lays down the model of game-ification in social media spaces that tempers how we speak about social justice and oppression and how we interact with one another. Courage is about being willing to enforce rules of engagement and set clear expectations, knowing that this may result in fewer "friends," likes, shares, clicks, and all of the hoped-for affirmations that such things entail.

Courage is speaking clearly about issues of import to us as people of faith without resorting to attacking people who disagree. Prophetic witness is never popular, but we are called to share the perspective of our faith tradition on the issues that most press us today. And we should be able to do so without fear.

It takes courage to be a peacemaker, to disrupt the narratives of empire, and to refuse to participate in acts of vilification and outrage that so frequently occur in the social media space. It takes courage to call out injustice without shaming those who perpetrate it or have yet to figure out the ways in which they participate in it.

It also takes courage to speak openly of our faith in public spaces, and social media is no exception. Bearing witness to alternatives to the systems of aggression and coercion that destroy the dignity of God's people is a part of our Christian calling. As potentially one of the most influential communities we belong to, one that most of us visit and interact with on some level every day, it is a sad fact that too many of us are reluctant to express our faith in that forum. Perhaps this is because we are afraid of being branded as fanatical, or perhaps this is because there is no end of contemporary anxiety about religion that is freely vented in the digital world. But we are told to not be afraid. We should heed this.

Courage means running a risk each time we try to diffuse a conflict online, remind one another to keep our engagements respectful, or enforce boundaries and expectations in our own curated space. Courage means risk every time we call out unjust systems, point out marginalization, and give voice to alternative viewpoints on the prevailing social or political narratives. And just as quietness doesn't give us license as Christians to remain silent in the face of injustice, courage also doesn't give us license to simply assert our thoughts and opinions without regard to the ways in which they may harm. Courage, like quietness, gives us space to discern whether our thoughts on a given subject are necessary or merely self-indulgent.

Prayer

Finally, we come to prayer. The beginning and the end of our lives as Christian disciples. It is everything in between. It can be said, in fact, that it is the very model of our relationship with God and one another that is demonstrated over and over again in the life of Jesus in the Gospels. So how is prayer a virtue for our social media witness? Perhaps *prayerful-ness* is a better word, but that is a posture rather than an act of faith that can alter our engagement with those we have friended. I submit that prayer is an essential act that belongs in our social media space. Not just the offering of prayers for the benefit of others, but the use of them to temper our own perspectives and interactions. When I write lengthy posts (something which I am too often accused of doing), I pray before I write them, while I write them, before I post them, and as I witness reactions to them.

We are often asked to pray by and for others on social media. And we should do so. I'm not talking about the "type AMEN if you agree" messages or prayer chains contained in overly sentimental memes that subtly (or not so subtly) guilt people into sharing if they want to be seen as faithful Christians. I mean the honest-to-goodness self-offering that is prayer. Why are we often afraid to do this? Prayer changes our hearts and sometimes the hearts of others.

As a Christian, when I tell people I will pray for them, I am not intruding into their own faith life or their particular beliefs (or lack of them). I am neither being superstitious nor meddlesome. What I am doing, as a person of faith, is letting them know I am offering myself intimately—the most intimate way I know how, in fact—to their concerns and cares. It is a part of my Christian vocabulary that I need not be reticent about or apologetic. My prayer is a willingness to connect with others by sharing in their pains and fears.

Sooner or later, as people of faith we have to come to the conclusion that our faith is intended to draw us into deeper relationship with others—to share with one another in the burdens of our human frailty, our joys and tears, and our laughter and frustrations. Prayer is the way in which we learn to do this. And it is important for us as Christian people to bring this essential part of our discipleship into our whole lives. It is likely way past time that we let go of our reticence to do so in a social media landscape.

5

So, Now What?

How do we remain faithful disciples in the social media space? This is an increasingly important question. Here we have explored the benefits of social media, from its global reach to its capacity for interaction with a great variety of people and perspectives. We have learned to accommodate the realities of real-time interaction and the joy of connection it brings. Its promise of exposing us to great cultural diversity and helping us discover shared values is nearly unprecedented in any other modern technological innovation. There are so many benefits to this global phenomenon.

Along with the joys, however, we also know that there are a great many challenges, not the least of which is the possible diminishment of actual relationships due to a model of interaction that is merely an approximation of reality and is too often merely transactional.

As Christian disciples, there is an imperative for us to be responsible "curators" or stewards of our social media space, whether our Twitter feed, our Facebook timeline, or any other space we maintain. This often means setting boundaries and expectations about what behavior is appropriate in the spaces we hold.

To counteract this false model of relationship, we must make efforts to foster relationships outside of the social media platforms we engage in. This means reclaiming the term "friend" and separating it from online followers who merely consume. We must be mindful of our capacity to reinforce our own biases and narratives by culling out those with whom we disagree and the creation of silos where we only hear views that don't challenge us.

To do this, we must begin to rediscover the art of conversation and all that is entailed in the authentic presence of ourselves with others. We must remember the personhood and dignity of those with whom we interact and to appreciate anew the voices and values of others that may differ from our own.

A tool for this new way of bringing our full Christian discipleship into the social media landscape is to remember the world between screens, where the Spirit is given space in her role as *God as Observer* and we can begin to reassert and respect the humanity of the person on the other end of a virtual interaction.

It is my hope that we have begun to explore a very rudimentary ethic for our witness on social media. Quietness, patience, humility, charity, courage, and prayer—this is far from an exhaustive list of the virtues we might use to frame our presence as Christian disciples both in the world of social media and more broadly in real life. However, these virtues are a good starting place for serving as witnesses of God's unbounded love.

I believe these character qualities will help foster the growth and stability of prayerful spiritual communities online. But above all, we must begin from the proposition that social media challenges will not be overcome if we *don't* bring these virtues with us. It is fine to occasionally lament the poor quality of interactions that occur in the digital landscape—the diminishment of authentic dialogue; the lack of real information; and the seemingly lost capacity for and disintegration of love, patience, and kindness in human interactions are all realties that we must grapple with. But it is most important that we begin to understand our role in changing this. As followers of the Prince of Peace, it is time for us to bring the depth of our spiritual selves with us into the virtual space and allow it to inform how we engage with platforms that are powerful enough to shape the world.

Happy posting, tweeting, snapchatting, and messaging! Remember the power of words and images to heal or to harm, and give witness to the love of the Redeemer with joy. I wish you peace.